HE
INVENTION
OF
MONSTERS
/
PLAYS
FOR
THE
THEATRE

The Invention of Monsters / Plays for the Theatre
© 2015 C Dylan Bassett

Published by Plays Inverse Press
Pittsburgh, PA
www.playsinverse.com

ISBN 13: 978-0-9914183-2-9

First Printing: April 2015
Cover design by Chelsea Majuri
Page design by Tyler Crumrine
Printed in the U.S.A.

PLAYS
INVERSE

# THE INVENTION OF MONSTERS / PLAYS FOR THE THEATRE

C DYLAN BASSETT

PLAYS INVERSE PRESS
PITTSBURGH, PA
2015

"The face has a great future, but only if it is destroyed, dismantled."

— Deleuze and Guattari

"I am large, I contain multitudes."

— Walt Whitman

*For Kylan*

# CONTENTS

# THE
# INVENTION
# OF
# MONSTERS

ONE
ACT

[SCENE]

The face is the initial uncertainty, the first of many wrong answers. The concept of one exists within us as the concept of something, a matchstick, for example: one catalogues two— one matchstick fits into two matchsticks. You are not you here, etc. Horses vanish in the west without anyone to notice, the sea plashes mildly. A boy at a certain age is mistaken for a girl. Masturbating, I am surprised how easily everything bleeds.

[SCENE]

When I was still a fetus my mother told me the wrong stories.
This is the cock, this is the screw. "Oneself" meaning one's
place in line. Men abandon ship, dragonflies unfurl their
long fingers to take us away. I assume the position in white
socks. Almost all of my friends are dressed in neckties. The
field is nearly dark. I am the man the man declined to be.
Unwelcome to the club.

[SCENE]

The woman, the baby, the bedroom. In certain social settings, one defers casually to ready-made hierarchies. I have said nothing about the woman, nor her relationship to the baby. Neither have I mentioned to whom the room belongs, nor what happened there. We make weather simply believing in it. The self occurs but only as proxy. I have said nothing about the man who does not speak to the woman so much as flex his tongue.

[SCENE]

When the music ends the stranger appears on stage in a suit of human hair. The shock of nudity, the actual body. Now that I'm here I could be anyone. (Carnivorous I. I of the graven image.) The role of the boy is played by a skeleton inside a smaller boy. The old woman is played by a younger woman with white hair. Wind is defined as a crooked line, a voice of various proportions. Birds explode into smaller birds.

[SCENE]

Nothing's the cause of these clouds. I've endured my life as a man in another man's image. I watch the moon in an empty bowl where the moon is floating. The headache ensues. Whether in bed or at sea, love is simple. Two boats abob in gray sink water. Rain falls into the teacup. I'm coming into my own.

[SCENE]

A slow dance where we touch each other's boats. The fingernails shimmer in the toilet bowl. The sequins float out with the tide. A wine glass resembles a woman in a dress, or a child's swimming pool into which the child is bleeding. The audience cheers when the wounded body addresses them directly. My face is a mirror, other faces come and go.

## [SCENE]

The plot does not occur in sequence but in various sampled geographies. A boy becoming a man becomes a lady all over again. It's a businessman's sadness. It's getting lost on purpose. I'm in love with whatever's inside that gorilla suit. I'm a deer with all of its lights on. I lie down in the trash and it does not hurt. I reach for my penis but find a piece of fruit. Or, never mind.

[SCENE]

These are not my cheekbones but I wear them like I always
do. I am the tiny person inside my skull. One of us sees the
other through a window. I am not yet used to being alive. The
world is plastic grapes. Death can be whatever in hindsight.
A light shining 24 hours on a parking lot, a mountain in a
swimming pool, a tuna fish sandwich laced with hooks. You
misunderstand, my funny demon voice is my real voice.

[SCENE]

The clouds have blown. The police dogs enter the stage like bad ideas. Being taller, I play the man's role. I unwrap my scarf to reveal the cause of grief is looking at a face. An onion peeled beneath water. When the dream concludes the feelings continue. Love might be terror. Sex might be werewolf, etc. It's dark out there and someone's in it.

[SCENE]

I put on the nightmare hands. I pretend myself back to life.
I put on the correct suit and feel the correct feeling. Are they
bat people or real people? So much meat, so much clothing.
The landscape and the language are the same sensory
derangement. Loosely a fox hatches from a chicken egg.

[SCENE]

Moreover, the stage has vanished. A little boy dances beneath no music. Compassion and cruelty are natural responses to the same basic problem. Fake blizzard, real prayer. Memories occur in flashes but more frequently. I am the only child in my childhood, my only friend is a matchstick. I pretend to be a pirate then become one. I eat alone and become my age. Don't look! A vampire mask made from a paper plate.

[SCENE]

I love you makes me wonder who is you and who is I. I run in the rain or the rain is running. Go to the mirror and see for yourself if you don't believe it. Even before I was named I had this voice inside me. A nail inside a jar of honey.

[SCENE]

At this point, the players lift up their cut-off genitalia. Some things are better said in public. A nightmare is a phenomenon of the physical world, including plants, animals, landscapes, and other products of the earth. Silence settles on the child's playroom. I worry but over-wait. I wear my father's mouth because mine got messed up. It's something for the audience to laugh at. A horse rides another horse.

[SCENE]

A boy who is a girl is an elephant by default. The traffic lights blink to indicate a malfunction. No one is crying. The entire future is bright with red.

[SCENE]

The bathtub overflows into the dream. The bed is always empty with me in it. I locate my hands downriver. My hands are piano music. I live inside a photograph of myself with a bloody lip. I live inside a boy and we live together out of context. I am knives wrapped in yellow hair. I build ghosts out of a body.

[SCENE]

How gentle the lamplight, how green the star. I'm fine to die here, says the weatherman. Everyone is human who doesn't feel like it. I have hammers for hands and am labeled accordingly. When my sister was a little girl she was a boy, and therefore forbidden to touch anything. Loneliness vs. average rain. The universe is eye sockets. I peel a banana and find a small yellow finger inside.

## [SCENE]

A man wanting to be beautiful puts on a dress whereas a woman wanting power takes one off. The cougar mounts the deer. The boy walks into the ocean and finds an ocean. The priest runs from room to room in pursuit of a better book. The point of the story is, what else can we disown? Does the boy make it home and under whose maim? In hell we cannot tell people from other people. I cannot remember whom I have loved.

[SCENE]

There isn't much time. My fingernails grow even as I say this. People dump their trash in the desert. The night is dark, the knife is dark. There is no clock but I think I hear a bird. There is the carcass of a dog left on the highway beneath whose skin another child is born.

# FANTASIES ABOUT COWBOYS

ONE
ACT

[SCENE]

The cowboy appears on stage as if by chance. As if by chance the audience applauds. You're more likely to be killed by your own father, says the father. I strip down to bones and I am what I was. How many cocks inside one cowboy? It feels like I'm smiling but I'm not. To suppress my sex drive I pull out leg hair in the shower. A helicopter hacks a radio tower.

[SCENE]

Now that the politicians are here, the sex can begin. The men start their engines. They remove their hats as if at church. A cut flower bleeds down the throat of a bottle. Already I know too many things by what they are named. Imagine a world where everyone plays with dolls. I'm only shaped like a man. The eye holds prisoner what it beholds. Seeing a hole in the ground, I see myself.

[SCENE]

An ill wind that blows nothing, autumn downloads its leaves. It's hard enough to understand the sequence of things: the queen is handled by the king, the king by the court jester, etc. No face is new. No face emits light. Those who surrender must. Look and see how men conduct themselves around their would-be lovers. You cannot dream about love until you've made it. It's a bloody mess but it's about to get bloodier.

[SCENE]

We finally have sex but forget to remove our Halloween masks. A stranger watches through the black slats of a chair. A nightmare, a small community or group of houses. It's quiet in the world, the whole of you inside me. One would like to know the context of this story. Someone's Jesus reaches for a gun.

[SCENE]

There are many people on earth and most of them are dead. Also there are soldiers. A couple walks arm in arm, a boy and a girl, as far as I can tell, being led to the slaughterhouse. Accidents happen again. When the actors remove their clothing, we cannot remember whom to pity, whom to blame.

[SCENE]

In an act of complete physical subjection, the pupil allows the professor to plunge his knife. When the elevator goes down it is for good. The maid is in her bed, doing what beds are good for. A doll is passed from boy to boy at a campsite, the noise of sharp scissors cutting. By a blade I am disrobed. Beneath my robe a sexier robe.

[SCENE]

Hair grows away from the flesh, but quietly as if wanting to escape. Memory prefigures perspective, the child gropes at the nipple's machine. In my memory, memory. Aren't the women beautiful beneath their umbrellas? Most people assume everything is about sex. A play within a play: you can watch but you cannot intervene. I fall in love without even trying. No Americans were hurt.

[SCENE]

The kid takes the candy, the batter takes the pitch. After much anticipation and some embarrassment, the long wait for the sex doll ends and the man begins to rearrange its various body parts as one might rearrange a puzzle, an anatomical mapping. He raises her arms, for example, to cover her mouth. Everywhere the smell of wet and heavy feathers. The hand mirror reveals a capsized ship. No less than instinct is the cannibalism of the crickets. It's a bad habit, wanting to understand. Toys bob in a swimming pool.

## [SCENE]

Selfhood foregrounds a sense of geography. The hills are said to be breasts and the cowboy lies down. At any given time one is simply being oneself. One person is many, each a potential hero. I am erasing what I can. When I said "me" I meant "she," though little else in daily life goes unauthorized. I grow up and ghastly. You have a choice between pornography and riddles. The dread of seeing or being seen.

[SCENE]

Naming is a system in which I am subject to a constant "No." Meanwhile, my wife is shaving her legs and my husband is slicing a lemon. Community is not meant to protect us so much as expose us to others. The pronoun is the quickest method of identification. The moon may appear to move but it is I who am moving. The presence of a mirror elicits shame.

[SCENE]

Form is an event. Girls and boys exchange their parts in the foreground. Violence occurring in nature is natural, says the philosopher. Close your eyes, it hurts less if you close your eyes. Not even birds know where they're going or why. I am sorry for what I've done.

[SCENE]

My hands continue to grow which worries me because women are thought to have small hands, which also worries me because I am not a woman. Dancing also saddens us, says the executioner. Says the lover, I am gigantic. I am so glad you are here. There is no further need for horror films. What we cannot remember is of little use to us now. A sound like paper being torn.

[SCENE]

Approaching climax, the boy looks up like an animal drinking. The desires to build and to break are equal, a nightmare where people finally understand each other. The swan reflects a rhinoceros, the brutal ritual of becoming. When I look at the audience I am the audience. When I hold the knife I feel like using it. I am not what I wished for. Call me footless. The red dress girl, neither home nor lost.

# SCENES
# OF
# HEROISM

ONE
ACT

[SCENE]

The sentence begins in terror. The soldier wakes up and I am him. It takes years of practice to put a war inside a thimble. Tightly the planet turns away. A new unfamiliar landscape can make a prior unfamiliar landscape feel like home. A fire is framed before it's photographed. There is order in the life of boys and men. I know because I am here. Exit is only a sign.

[SCENE]

Blood on the sock on the snow on the car. We are what the war stands for. The flies take the skies. The smoke is not dense enough to hide what we do not want to see. The president fingers his violin, his certainty still intact. Power manifests itself in probable tasks. Policemen guide traffic. Money changes hands.

[SCENE]

I find love in the mouth of a bat. The clown laughs at the moon and the soldier cries for a similar reason. This is the opposite of finding your voice. This is the opposite of "anything could happen." What do I look like before my parents are born? And what does a bat love? My head is a room in which my parents are always dying, never dead.

[SCENE]

Thrust into conversation the elephants are born. This sun is "killing me." More often than not simple solutions guide our actions, a gunshot begets a war begets a gunshot. In their gowns, the saints are easily murdered. The ocean sloshes in the smallish pitcher. A soul is just a radio. Choose carefully your victim.

[SCENE]

Another corpse and someone there to take a picture. No blood but red worms. One thousand tiny sex organs. Things make more sense beneath a river. I should be born before I say anything else. I should comb my hair. I sleep with the windows open to scare away the strangers. My clothing eats my skin. Home requires everyone's imagination. I will know what's lost when I find it. None of this will help.

[SCENE]

As if they are not men, photographs with the heads cut out. I walk where once there was a garden. I get so lonely walking. I wear all the bodies I love. When I see the gnawed torso of a rabbit, I get the feeling I'm eating it. The spirit is alive in the building. On the day the soldier is shot, a woman spills wine on a white dress. A piano plays itself in an empty mall. The weather holds.

[SCENE]

The trees tremble like men and women undressing. The dancer dances despite the blood gathering in her shoe. Even now warfare is given to obvious motifs: brainwashing, torture, who chases whom. The jungle is soldiers in jungle camouflage. My toes tear my shoes. All babies look normal under a modified lighting.

[SCENE]

Tall buildings watch me while I work. A swarm of bees becomes a pack of wolves when they die. The arrow snatches the hat from my head before I can imagine it. The priests protest what they can in prayer. I raise my cupped hands until all they hold is each other. The flags are gone but not the wind.

## [SCENE]

The morning struggles to assert itself. The rifle takes its aim. The dim crow dissolves into the eye of the cat. Statistics have replaced mythology, information is the story I sing myself. Even tied to a dock a raft travels thousands of miles. Whatever hasn't happened never will. A painter paints herself out of the landscape. Nowhere is the past. Even more broken glass.

# A
# TENT
# FOR
# THE
# NIGHT

ONE
ACT

[SCENE]

Order is restored to the earth once more, the giant quid
propels itself slowly and majestically through the deep.
I vomit on Sunday. I feel like part of something bigger.
Religion is framed as a reversal of fortune. A magic in which
very little disappears. In haste and in love, the lovers swallow.
The faithful proceed. The cruel hand descends once more
into its glove.

[SCENE]

When the smoke kicks up I put on my gray coat. The gods have lost their names. The symbolism of the dove depends on its color, no current photo available. I am all of me muscular action figures. I dream the giant staircase. I touch the mud and I am made of it. Language cannot tell the truth. Come home safely.

## [SCENE]

Sensual garden, oncoming train. Gradually, I learn time. Again I learn it, a dark figure in a contradicting light. When I am a boy God is a little taller, but never real. A new screw made to measure in advance. A girl inside of a boy inside of a baby. Guilt is invoked when one part of an interdependent unit falls short of an inherited history. Trash floats toward no conclusion. Everyone is alone but how no one can say.

[SCENE]

Men fuck the earth to make it fertile. Women lift their skirts
to let it rain. Where do I fit in? I wanted to be touched by
God not knowing I already had been. Death is always new. A
moth gets caught in a keyhole.

[SCENE]

Some men and some women made in the image of God. In part this is because many people are content with existing reciprocity. The wet bird flicks past, the hand has waved. God walks into a man and a baby goes to sleep. The hunter shoots the deer over and over, but the deer won't die. Look at anything long enough and you begin to imitate it. To love something you must carry it on your back.

[SCENE]

A crowd of figures is a figure in motion. A little beast child
eats oranges in the middle of the street. No ghosts left to
astonish us. I secure my mask before assisting others. I touch
my eyes so as to remember. I cross out the oceans. A shark
among sharks. Nobody is by herself. A city tall enough to
mute the sun.

[SCENE]

A face in the dark is the size of the dark. Unzipping his pants, an air of finality. Holiness is a matter of precedence, men kiss men exactly. I fall to my knees in tender despair. A prayer, ready for a blow. An exhale that requires additional violence. Fear is what the sign says. The child expiring becomes the adult. A finger grows painfully inside her. Somewhere a house collapses. Nothing shouts back.

[SCENE]

The world's as dark as someone painted it. A hawk eats its own wings. A man in a cat suit kills an actual cat. No one knows how the weapons got here and no one asks. My mouth is all bandages. (Where is the doctor. Someone get the doctor.) There's something to be afraid of, says the man with the megaphone. The man looks like my father but he is not. He wears my father's shirt.

[SCENE]

The sun sets vaguely on the newborn babe. The airplane glides parallel to the miniature dragonfly. Night means eyes inside a mouth. Was it raining while I dreamed? It happens that I get tired of being a man and become dogs chewing corners off the house. Aspirin unravels in a glass of water. Totally self-contained is what we call beautiful. All that technology for naught.

**ABOUT**

C Dylan Bassett is a teaching fellow at the Iowa Writers'
Workshop. His poems have been published in *Ninth Letter*,
*The Journal*, *Sonora Review*, *Verse Daily*, and elsewhere.

**ACKNOWLEDGMENTS**

Some of these scenes, often in different forms, have been published in *Ampersand Review*, *Apartment*, *Atlas Review*, *Birdfeast*, *Black Warrior Review*, *Bodega*, *Columbia Poetry Review*, *Copper Nickel*, *DIAGRAM*, *elsewhere journal*, *H_NGM_N*, *Hobart*, *Inter/rupture*, *Laurel Review*, *Mid-American Review*, *Ninth Letter*, *Pinwheel*, *Salt Hill*, *TENDERLOIN*, and *West Branch*. Thank you to all these editors.

Several of these pieces also appeared in the chapbooks *Some Futuristic Afternoons* (Strange Cage, 2014) and *The Invention of Monsters / A Performance in One Act*, co-written with Summer Ellison (iO Books, 2014). Thank you to Russell Jaffe, Wendy Xu, and Kyle McCord.

A special thanks to Riley Bassett, Eric Baus, Tyler Crumrine, Matthew Fee, Carolina Ebeid, David Greenspan, William Jameson, Richard Kenney, Hannah Loeb, Chelsea Majuri, Fatima Mirza, Jack Murphy, D.A. Powell, Joseph Sherlock, Donna Stonecipher, G.C. Waldrep, and Elizabeth Willis, for their support and insight regarding this project.

I am particularly grateful to Emma Winsor Wood, for her unceasing encouragement and love.